Your First

Best-Seller Book

Inside Secrets from a #1 Best-Selling Author

Sandra Brazelton

Foreword

I am a lifetime learner. I believe that every age and stage of our lives provides powerful learning opportunities.

I believe that we are all part of nature so we must continue to grow.

I believe God blesses each of us with infinite intellect and unlimited capacity.

I believe God created us to share His blessings and to serve others.

Writing a book provides the perfect vehicle to share the best of you.

I also believe that most of us suppress our genius when we should embrace it.

Writing a book releases your greatness to the Universe.

Pulitzer Prize-winning novelist Jane Smiley is quoted as saying that "writing is an Exercise in Freedom." 1

My prayer is that this book inspires you to take action so you can leave a timeless legacy for future generations to enjoy. To God be the Glory!

Dedication

There is more in what you know than what you do.

Therefore, this book is dedicated to those who choose to become lifetime learners and who have the courage and audacity to share that knowledge with others.

I also believe in the laws of attraction so you are not reading this by coincidence.

You obviously have the desire which must germinate and grow into action.

Your First Best-Seller Book is designed to take you by the hand and to help you share your wisdom, passion, purpose, intellect, and information with the Universe. Go Get It!

About the Author

Sandra Brazelton – CEO, MBA

Sandra Brazelton is a CEO, consultant, government contractor, author, retired engineer, 30-year entrepreneur, and real estate broker.

She is the Entrepreneur of the Year for several organizations.

She is also a proud graduate of Leadership Huntsville with a strong background in executive leadership and community service.

Her instructor credentials include certifications from the state of Alabama.

She also trained as part of her job description as a civil service engineer.

She is a motivational speaker, author, and empowerment thought leader.

Her website is www.sandrabrazelton.com.

Contents

FOREWORD I

DEDICATION III

ABOUT THE AUTHOR V

INTRODUCTION 1

15 STEP CONTENT ORGANIZATIONAL STRATEGY 5

PAID PUBLISHER VS. SELF-PUBLISH 11

10 CRITERIA FOR CHOOSING A PUBLISHER 13

YOUR FIRST BOOK BUDGET...15

YOUR OUTLINE IS YOUR ROADMAP 17

FIRST IMPRESSIONS 19

THE TITLE TELLS IT ALL! 21

MARKETING...23

WRITE IT RIGHT...25

EDITING YOUR BEST SELLER 27

A PICTURE PAINTS A THOUSAND WORDS 31

12 STEPS TO WRITE A #1 BEST SELLER 33

COMPENSATION 35

SUMMARY 37

MORE INSPIRING BOOKS 39

REFERENCES 43

Introduction

Photo by <u>Kourosh Qaffari</u> on <u>Unsplash</u>

"In all my life, I have never been free. I have never been able to do anything with freedom, except in the field of my writing."

Langston Hughes (1)

Great books transform lives, liberate our minds, empower the underserved, strengthen countries, guide others, challenge our imagination, embellish us with wisdom, teach us, and uplift our morality.

Becoming an author gives you instant credibility and subject matter expertise status.

It is a deeply fulfilling, personal accomplishment that opens doors, and provides endless opportunities.

Truly, it is worth the work.

However, writing a book and becoming a #1 Best-selling author are worlds apart.

The distinction of being a #1 Best-selling author is a higher and more exclusive level of achievement and success. This is evidenced by the fact that millions of books are written, yet very few achieve this distinction.

Writing a #1 best-seller is both rewarding and challenging.

The largest barriers may lie deep inside of you. This could be fear, procrastination, poor work ethic, excuses, and the lack of self-discipline, and self-motivation to finish what you start.

Our goal is to pull back the curtains and provide the insights, tips, motivation, and strategies that I used to become a #1 best-selling author, and to self-publish multiple books in different genres.

We step you through the entire maze from organizing to publishing. We also provide lessons learned and recommendations for cover creators, publishers, etc. so you can benefit from our extensive research. I also provide pro tips and links to several of my books so you can see the finished product.

Imagine the personal pride and sense of accomplishment that you will feel. As a #1 Best-selling author, your peers will recognize you as a subject matter expert and industry leader.

We know that new authors have a lot of questions and we want to help you avoid the pitfalls. "Your First Best-Seller Book" is the blueprint to help you publish, profit, and avoid the pitfalls of becoming a #1 best-selling author. It will save you time, money, anxiety, and stress while motivating you to publish "Your First Best-Seller Book."

We are thankful and excited to guide you through this journey.

15 Step Content Organizational Strategy

Photo by Josh Hild on Unsplash

Desire is the number one characteristic for success.

My first book is entitled "Wills, Probate, and Real Estate – What you Don't Know Can Cost You Thousands."

As a 30-year real estate broker and instructor, I was truly motivated to write this book so I could help families prepare for and retain generational wealth after the death of a loved one. It also distinguished me as a subject matter expert to help with probate sales.

I already had the information and the passion so the challenge was to organize the book and to make it user-friendly.

I remember spending the Thanksgiving holiday preparing the content using a Word file on my computer to organize the content. My goal was to begin with the end in mind and to answer the questions that I thought would be relevant to my target audience.

Avoid the Pitfalls

Completing a book requires a lot of self-discipline, self-motivation, and commitment. Most new authors start off with excitement and fizzle out before they finish.

Fortunately, there are phone and computer applications that can help you. Some of them will translate your oral content into a written format for you. This can save you a lot of time, money, and anxiety.

However, you must avoid distractions and command the self-discipline and focus that this serious endeavor requires.

Regardless of how you choose to develop the content, you must have a strong desire with accountability so you will have the motivation to focus and finish what you start.

You can always find an excuse to stop or quit. However, your desire must be stronger than any perceived barriers to your success.

Pro Tip

Many writers never complete their book because they continue to add content.

They fall into the writer's abyss and end up drowning in content that overwhelms them.

Do not think you must include all of the content in your first book. You can always update the book with your next edition.

These are the 15 questions for you to answer that will help you organize your book.

I also used this checklist to develop the content.

Please examine these questions closely and document your answers carefully.

1. What is your motivation?

2. Are you a subject matter expert?

3. Do you have experience in what you are sharing?

4. Who are you talking to?

5. Why are you talking to them?

6. Why should they listen to you?

7. Who is your ideal customer?

8. What do they look like?

9. What do they do for a living?

10. Where do they live?

11. What is their background?

12. How old are they?

13. How do they think?

14. What do you want them to know?

15. What action do you want them to take?

Based on this organizational strategy outline, I chose a workbook format and used expertise from attorneys and contributors to strengthen and validate the content

Paid Publisher vs. Self-publish

Photo by Arif Riyanto on Unsplash

One of the first decisions you must make is should you hire a publisher or should you self-publish. I performed a great deal of research and due diligence in this area so I could make the best decision.

10 Criteria for Choosing a Publisher

This is a summary of the 10 Criteria I looked for when choosing my publisher:

1. Established Publisher

2. Experience with the genre of real estate

3. Strong expertise in all aspects of publishing

4. Ability to set publishing schedule with accountability

5. Reasonable cost for services

6. Ability to communicate and track each step of the process

7. Infrastructure to promote the book to #1 Best-seller status

8. Value-added benefits

9. Reliable references to other services

10. Familiarity with using the Amazon publishing platform

Based on my research, I chose Prominence Publishing - suzanne@prominencepublishing.com. Although my publisher lived in another country (Canada), we were able to use email, phone, and video conferencing to effectively communicate and to accomplish all of the objectives.

Most importantly, the lessons I learned were the springboard to the multiple books that I have self-published.

Your First Book Budget

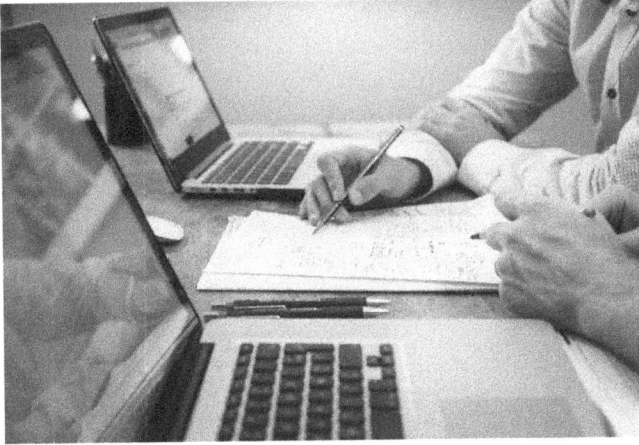

Most authors choose self-publishing because they think it is less expensive. However, do not make that decision based on price alone. There are many other factors to consider such as time, quality, success, accountability, and marketability of your finished book.

In addition, your expertise is as a content-provider, not a graphics designer or editor.

The other fact is that you need a lot of self-motivation to finish a book. I know of writers who take years and years to finish a book because they procrastinate and they have no sense of priority or urgency. In this case, paying a publisher is a good investment because the money you pay will provide skin in the game to keep you focused and accountable.

These are the typical expenses of publishing a book:

- ➤ Research

- ➤ Outline

- ➤ Write

- ➤ Edit

- ➤ Format

- ➤ Cover

- ➤ Publish

- ➤ Market

My investment was close to $2,000.00 and it was well worth it. My publisher worked with my budget and allowed me to perform some of my own tasks. She provided the ISBN/barcode, 3D book covers, references for editors, formatters, press releases, graphics, etc. She also helped me navigate the kdp.amazon.com technology portal.

The publisher's support was invaluable. Her expertise allowed me to go from manuscript to book signing in sixty days with a #1 Best-Seller.

Your Outline is Your Roadmap

Photo by Glenn Carstens-Peters on Unsplash

This is a traditional outline for a book. Some sections may apply and some may not. This book has an example of many of these sections.

- ✓ Title

- ✓ Copyright

- ✓ Dedication

- ✓ Acknowledgements

- ✓ Use Contributors

- ✓ Foreword

- ✓ Contents

- ✓ Introduction

- ✓ Chapters

- ✓ Appendix

- ✓ FAQ – Frequently Asked Questions

- ✓ Support

- ✓ Contributors

- ✓ Reference

- ✓ About Author

- ✓ Legal Release

Pro Tip

Most writers never finish their book because they continue to add content. Their goal is to have the perfect book. However, this is an unrealistic expectation because there is no such thing as a perfect book. Remember, you can always update your book with multiple editions. My suggestion is to write a draft summary first and to stop when you have 85% of the content.

First Impressions

Before

After

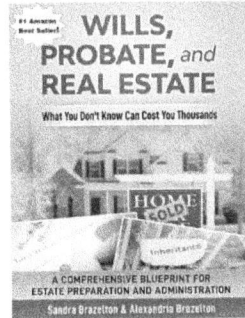

The cover of your book is the first thing readers see. Therefore, the colors, fonts, and layout must be attractive. I recommend that you research different book covers and invest in a professional company to design your cover.

Look at the two covers above. Both of them have the exact same content. Which one of these books would you consider just based on the cover? The one on the left is my design that I spent time and money developing, and the one on the right is the professional design by Pixelstudio. The Pixelstudio design has instant marketing and eye appeal that helped my book stand out from the competition. Clearly, I made a good decision by choosing them.

A professional cover is small investment that will help you become a #1 Best-selling author.

The Title Tells It All!

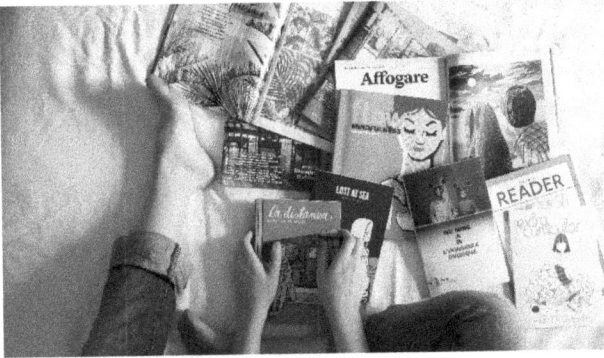

Photo by Giulia Bertelli on Unsplash

The most important parts of any book are the title and the cover.

The title draws attention and the cover is the face of the book.

In my opinion, this is where the focus and funds should be spent.

Remember, the title should be catchy, marketable, interesting, and a direct representation of the book. It should contain catchy phrases and alliterations.

Our title; Wills, Probate, and Real Estate, has good rhythm and also includes alliteration.

Also, the title should be easy to track using search engine optimization.

In order to choose this title, I researched similar titles using Google, Amazon, and other search engines.

The good news is titles do not have copyright protection.

Also, the subtitle refines the content and increases curiosity.

Our subtitle is "what you don't know can cost you thousands." This sub-title was intentionally selected to encourage the reader to choose our book. I have included a link to our other books in the reference so you can see how the title and subtitle move the reader to action.

Marketing

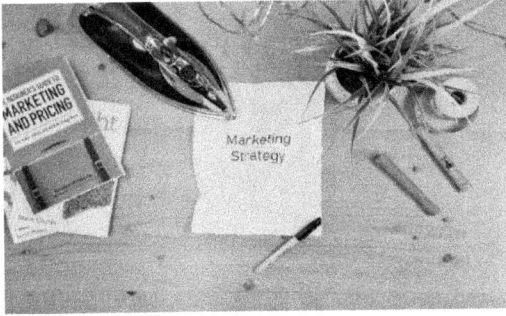

Photo by <u>Campaign Creators</u> on <u>Unsplash</u>

The sale of the book is not where the money is made so please price them reasonably.

The influence, relationships, status, opportunities, and connections are the revenue drivers.

Marketing can be online and in person.

My book launch was at our local church. I also share the author's link on my social media platforms.

Books are also great door prizes that you can donate to causes to help promote your brand. In addition, I provide books to other influencers at a discounted price so we can collaborate and they can profit from sharing the book.

Pro tip

Kdp.amazon.com will allow you to order author copies so you can have the final edit before it goes into print to be ordered.

Write it Right

Photo by Aaron Burden on Unsplash

Your book should be written based on your target audience. A high-technology book will have a different writing style than a book for first-time home buyers.

Also, the layout needs to make the content easy to read. My workbooks are sized 8.5x11 and the other ones are sized 6x9. I recommend an easy-to-read, simple writing style that goes from header to header in small chunks because this is how we have been trained to interpret information.

One of my biggest areas of frustration and rework is the format layout. Several of my books looked very different when I uploaded them in kdp.amazon.com.

The content was skewed and it looked very unprofessional. I obviously needed professional help and I have enjoyed the layout design from accuracy4sure on Fiverr.

Editing Your Best Seller

Photo by Kelly Sikkema on Unsplash

A quality and comprehensive edit is critical to the quality of your book. There is no substitute for a well-trained, objective eye; and no excuse for a book with a confusing layout that is filled with spelling and syntax errors.

Also, many new authors do not want to invest in a professional edit because they feel qualified to edit it themselves. It is very difficult for writers to edit their own work because their familiarity with the content allows errors to be easily over-looked.

These are the twelve editing steps that I use:

1. Edit for proper grammar

2. Edit for spelling

3. Edit for proper syntax

4. Edit for proper sentence structure

5. Edit for logical flow

6. Write in present tense

7. Edit to ensure all sources are properly referenced

8. Edit to ensure the graphics complement the content

9. Edit to ensure the information keeps the reader's attention

10. Read the book aloud

11. Ask others to critique it

12. Edit to update words and phrases that provide a more succinct and complete thought. For example:

    a. Before - "I never used an editor before and I am happy with the results."

    b. After – "My first experience with an editor was very rewarding."

Your #1 Best-Seller books will require strong, constructive, and rigorous edits.

You can research qualified editors on fiverr.com and other sites. When choosing an editor, check references and make sure the editor has experience in your field of expertise and genre.

In order to control the quality of Your First Best-Seller, you must provide the proper leadership and example to invest in multiple edits using qualified professionals.

A Picture Paints a Thousand Words

Photo by Jared Erondu on unsplash

Eighty percent of most readers are visual readers.

Visual Aids are power tools that help connect with readers who process information in different formats.

Therefore, pictures, charts, graphs, video, etc. really help with reader enjoyment and content retention.

There are many sites that provide free and royalty-free images such as flckr.com and unsplash.com.

You can also pay for a membership to different sites that provide graphics, videos, charts, etc.

However, please perform your own due diligence and make sure you provide proper credit to the image provider. You must also comply with   all   copyright   laws.

12 Steps to Write a #1 Best Seller

1. Develop a written outline

2. Choose a Powerful Title

3. Take control

4. Focus on Quality

5. Outsource cover design, editor, and layout services

6. Set a Deadline

7. Accept 85% accuracy

8. Begin with the end in mind

9. Make a strong, emotional connection

10. Use contributors to add value and social proof

11. Market

12. Consider professional public relations to promote your book

Pro Tip

Once the book is written, leave it alone for a few days and then read it again.

Follow the same process after major changes.

Save each version with a different date or revision number so you can track changes. The software can also track changes.

Compensation

Compensation is received from royalties, direct sales, and vendor relationships.

I used kdp.amazon.com to publish because they print the books as ordered and I am not burdened with the expense and management of stale inventory. They also provide an author site that helps drive traffic and demand. In addition, I reduced my upfront investment of time and capital tremendously by using their technology to publish and print.

Once the book is published, you can order author copies very reasonably based on the size of the book.

This allows you the flexibility to buy what you need or ship them directly to an event where you can sell them at retail. In addition, updates and changes are very easy to make. Also, the digital versions are very popular and provide higher royalties.

There is also a strong market demand for audio books.

Book sales are distributed and tracked through the International Standard Book Number (ISBN). Each ISBN comes with a unique number. ISBNs are required so that your book is distinguished from others and so you can receive proper credit and compensation.

On several of my self-published books, I used the ISBN and barcode provided by Amazon. However, I recently self-invested in my own ISBNs and barcodes from bowker.com so I can have wider distribution opportunities.

Summary

Writing is a powerful form of expression because it allows us to share ideas and document our memories.

Writing entertains, inspires, expresses, and motivates.

Writing frees the soul and takes us to places in our minds that stimulate our senses and awaken our imagination of possibilities.

Great writers challenge us, transform us, inform us, educate us, and inspire us.

Great writers provide facts, hope, instructions, excitement, and intrigue.

Great writers complete the pieces to the puzzles of our lives and encourage us to search for truth.

Without great writers there would be a hole in our souls and a void in our minds.

Your First Best-Seller Book is ready to launch from the creative thoughts of your mind to the pages of inspiration so you can mold it, refine it, and publish it.

The Universe deserves to hear what only you can tell.

Open your mind, free your imagination and write "Your First Best-Seller Book."

I hope you are inspired to use this blueprint to guide you through the success of "Your First Best-Seller Book."

More Inspiring Books

These are the links to additional books by Sandra Brazelton and her motivation for becoming a #1 Best-selling Author.

As an engineer, CEO, consultant, and entrepreneur, Sandra Brazelton has always broken down barriers. Therefore, her mission is to help you become your best you!

These books reflect her education in engineering and business, 30 years of experience, leadership, travel, training, and life experiences. Most importantly, based on her faith in God and study of His word, she has cracked the code to personal success.

She has met people from all over the world so she knows that the only race is the human race. She also believes that it is your birthright to succeed and that everything you need for success is already in you.

However, less than 3% of the world's population understand their inherent greatness and the Universal Principles of Wealth. The creative process is to pray, plan, and act. Her goal is to provide real world and relevant solutions to help you succeed. Her prayer is that these books will educate, inspire, and motivate you to unleash your inner warrior and enjoy the blessings of spirituality, health, and wealth that God empowered you to receive.

Wills, Probate, and Real Estate
What you don't know can cost you thousands
https://www.amazon.com/dp/1988925312

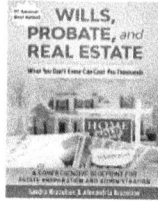

Online Real Estate Auctions
How to Build Wealth and Avoid Financial Disaster
https://www.amazon.com/dp/1796685747

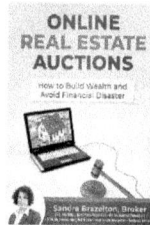

Live Your Purpose - 40 Point Guaranteed Success Blueprint

Your Spiritual Roadmap to Your Success Destination
https://www.amazon.com/dp/1090982755

Flip Don't Flop
Inside Secrets to Build Real Estate Investment Wealth
https://www.amazon.com/dp/1698180071

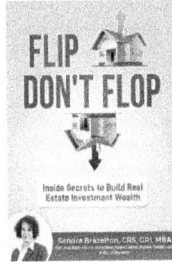

Mind Your Business:
55 Inside Secrets to Prevent Business Failure
https://www.amazon.com/gp/product/1658698827

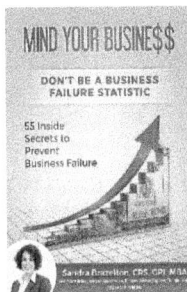

The CEO Blueprint for Diversity:
Inside Secrets to Lead, Understand, Prepare, and Thrive with Diversity
https://www.amazon.com/dp/1736068911

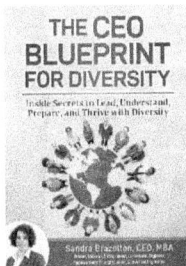

Money, Credit, and Wealth:

Spiritually-Based Financial Secrets to Build Generational Wealth

https://www.amazon.com/dp/1736068903

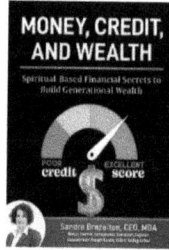

Your First Best-Seller Book

Inside Secrets from a #1 Best-Selling Author

https://www.amazon.com/dp/173606892X

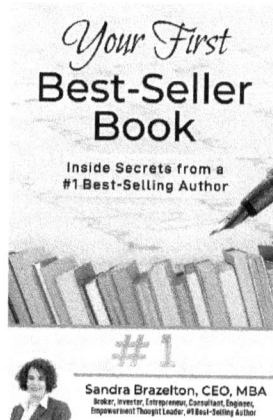

Pickleball For All

Inside Secrets for Fun, Safe, and Competitive Play

https://www.amazon.com/dp/B09792M5KS

References

1. https://www.mentalfloss.com/article/91742/20-inspiring-quotes-langston-hughes

2. https://www.theatlantic.com/entertainment/archive/2014/10/ideas-motivate-great-writing/381224/